CRYSTALLOGRAPHY

CHRISTIAN BÖK

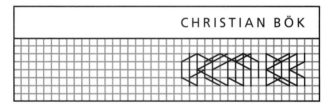

COACH HOUSE BOOKS

Published with financial assistance from the Canada Council
for the Arts and the Ontario Arts Council

The Canada Council   Le Conseil des Arts
      for the Arts   du Canada

ONTARIO ARTS COUNCIL
CONSEIL DES ARTS DE L'ONTARIO

NATIONAL LIBRARY OF CANADA
CATALOGUING IN PUBLICATION DATA

Bök, Christian, 1966–
        Crystallography / Christian Bök. – 2nd ed.

Poems.
ISBN 1-55245-119-4

        I. Title.

PS8553.O4727C7 2003   C811'.54   C2003-903471-2

for
the angel
in
the angle

Crystallographers ... have opened the gate that gives access to a vast land, but they themselves have not entered for they are by nature more interested in the means by which to open the portal rather than in the domain that lies beyond it....

Long ago during my wanderings, I happened to chance upon the neighbourhood of this domain. I saw a high wall, and because I had a presentiment of some enigma that might be hiding behind it, I climbed the wall with difficulty. On the other side, I landed in a wilderness through which I had to make my way with much effort until I arrived via detours at the open gate – the open gate of mathematics, from which many clear paths extended in all directions....

Sometimes I think that I have explored this entire garden, that I have trodden all its paths, and that I have admired all its views, when all of a sudden I detect another new pathway, and once again I savour another new delight....

I spend time there in refreshing, but oppressive, loneliness.

The Regular Division of the Plane
M. C. Escher

PRELIMINARY SURVEY

THE HAGIOGRAPHY OF SNOW

EUCLID AND HIS MODERN RIVALS

PRELIMINARY SURVEY

CRYSTALS

A crystal is an atomic tessellation, a tridimensional
jigsaw puzzle in which every piece is the same shape.

A crystal assembles itself out of its own constituent
disarray: the puzzle puts itself together, each piece
falling as though by chance into its correct location.

> A crystal is nothing more
> than a breeze blowing sand
> into the form of a castle
> or a film played backwards
> of a window being smashed.

A compound (word) dissolved in a liquid
supercooled under microgravitational
conditions precipitates out of solution
in (alphabetical) order to form crystals
whose structuralistic perfection rivals
the beauty of machine-tooled objects.

An archæologist without any mineralogical
experience
might easily mistake a crystal
for the artificial product of a precision
technology.

A word is a bit of crystal in formation.

c r y s t a l s

a
s
t
r
a
l

s
a
l
t

c
a
s
t

a
s
t
r
a
y

AMETHYST

```
S I L I C O N
        X
        Y
O X Y G E N
        E
        N
```

sibylline orchid

oblivious

EXPERIMENT #1

1

Amethyst sugar
stains tapwater,

like the inkjet
spray of toner

on wet paper,
words but dust

dissolved away
so faint liquid

can transmute
at the chiming

of the teaspoon
into grape paint.

Supersaturation.

2

Surgical thread
dipped in slowly

cooling glasses
of warm seltzer

with its solute
at a high degree

of concentration
attracts stray

atoms in the way
a magnetic wire

grows a cluster
of iron filings.

Coprecipitation.

3

Textbooks teach
you that to lock

solutions in your
icebox overnight

can precipitate
from water, candy

on a cord, words
accreting meaning

so that the line
can end at last

in the sweetest
of stalactites.

Crystallization.

```
                        l           c
                    c r y s t a l       r
        c               r       t       y l
        r               y       t   c r y s t a l
        y l         c r y s t a l  i   r     t   t
c r y s t a l           r     t         c   y     a   t
r     t   t             y l a t t i c e   s     l   i
y     a   t   c r y s t a l               t         c
s     l   i   r     t   t             l a t t i c e
t         c   y     a   t   c r y s t a l       r
l a t t i c e   s     l   i   r         t         y l
    l       r     t         c   y   l     t   c r y s t a l
        y l a t t i c e   s   a       i   r     t   t
    c r y s t a l           r     t   t   c   y     a   t
    r     t   t             y l a t t i c e   s     l   i
    y     a   t   c r y s t a l  i         t         c
    s     l   i   r     t   t   c     l a t t i c e
    t         c   y l a t t i c e         l
l a t t i c e   s     l   i
    l               t         c
        l a t t i c e
            l
```

CRYSTAL LATTICE

FRACTAL GEOMETRY

1

Fractals are haphazard maps
that entrap entropy in tropes.

Fractals tell their raconteurs
to counteract at every point
the contours of what thought
recounts (a line, a plot): recant
the chronicle that cannot coil
into itself – let the story stray
off course, its countless details,
pointless detours, all en route
toward a tour de force, where
the here & now of nowhere is.

Don't ramble – lest you dream
about a random belt of words
brought to you by Mandelbrot.

2

Fractals are a pretty knotty
way to say: the length of any
coastline depends upon the
lengths to which a ruler goes.

A lost vacationer who strolls
along a beach patrols a spatial
breach between dimensions.

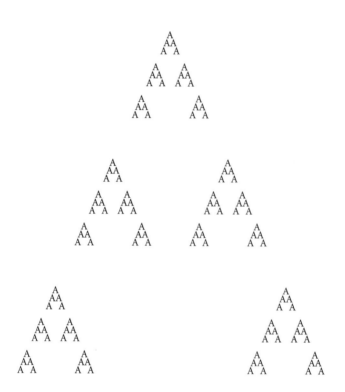

A-FRACTAL

3

A fractal is the ideal of redundancy:

> the obsessive restatement (re(in)statement)
> of itself, by itself, in itself – a never-ending
> message that digresses from its digressions
> yet nevertheless repeats (repeats) the same
> message over and over and over ad infinitum.

A fractal is the ideal of redundancy:

> imagine a series
> of Chinese boxes
> in which each box
> contains a series
> of Chinese boxes.

An acoustic fractal would be its own echo chamber.

4

Never forget that fractal
music sounds the same
when played at any speed.

Navigate the futile maze
this sentence plans to be.

Newfangle its simplicity.

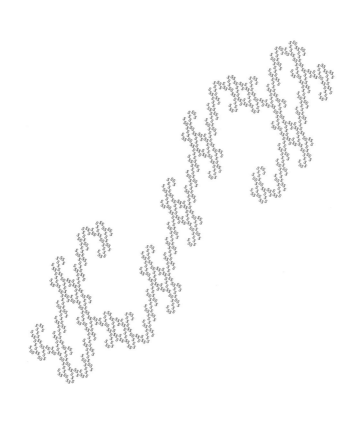

S-FRACTAL

5

When two identical mirrors face each other
their cycle of self-reflection recedes forever
into an infinite exchange of self-absorption.

Each mirror
infects itself
at every scale
with the virus of its own image.

Each mirror
devours itself
at every point
with the abyss of its own dream.

When we gaze upon a fractal, we must peer
at a one-way mirror, unaware of the other
mirror, standing somewhere far behind us.

6

Mirror rim (all its
sides reversed) is
still a mirror rim.

A fractal is a fatal
arc (an act as artful
as a fall): a snow-
flake knows a leaf.

K-FRACTAL

RUBY

```
              A
              L
              U
        A L U M I N U M
    O         I
    O X Y G E N
    Y         U
O X Y G E N   M
    E
    N
```

alizarine albedo

oriflamme, orchestrina
oxyacetylene

GLASS

Mercurial magma,
sand,
lime and soda
          cool
into a vitreous
solid,
the most viscous
          fluid,
a virtual liquid,
thick
enough to seem
          rigid:

fragile language.

Glass represents
a poetic element

exiled
to a borderline

between
states of matter:

breakable water

not yet frozen,

yet unpourable.

Chatoyant panes

in cathedral
windows flow
too slow
for eyes to see

illuminated
manuscripts
written
on glass pages,

bleeding away
ages of images.

Downward blur
of watercolour
sunsets,

melting
ink in thin
paraffin walls.

the windshield
dripping
like raindrops
upon it,
but more
incrementally.

Glass acoustics,
celestial music,

hyaline
instrumentarium:

verrillons, bottle
trees, armonicas,
and water gongs,

wet tambourines
and wind chimes,
icy glockenspiels
and clavicylinders.

Glass resonates
until shattered
by precise song.

Optic anomalies
magnify vision:

meaning, a form

of glassiness,

the misprision

of transparency.

EMERALD

```
                    O
                    X
                O   Y
                O X Y G E N
                  O   Y   E
                O X Y G E N
    C           O   Y   E
    H         O X Y G E N
    R   S       Y   E
    O   I       G   N
    M   L   E       B           S
S I L I C O N     B E R Y L L I U M
    U   C   X   B     R           L
    M   O X Y G E N   Y   S I L I C O N
        N   G   R     L   I     C   X
            E   Y     L   L       O X Y G E N
            N   L   S I L I C O N   G
                L     U   C   X     E
        A L U M I N U M   O X Y G E N
                U           N   G
                M       O       E
                    O X Y G E N
                  O   Y
                O X Y G E N
                    Y   E
                O X Y G E N
                    E
        A L U M I N U M
```

crownland beaumontage

sidereal
opulence of sinfulness

opaque, ornate, orphic

silkscreens of silent
orchards

oracular silviculture

alembic of silhouettes

bezels
oblique optics

berylloid observatory

alkali
octane, oxides

ozone overworld of oz

BIREFRINGENCE

See in silk-screened kimonos
blowtorch scars on metal,
wings of iridescent
insects,
the aurora borealis.

See in stained-glass windows
spotlight gels for sunlight,
broken slides of hoarfrost
crystals
magnified through polarizers.

See in gasoline rainbows
eyes plucked from peacock fans
fuelling dreams of burning
asphalt.
Words kaleidoscope together.

Houseflies
see the world through gemstones.

CRYSTALS

A crystal makes a lens through which a Cubist
painter might see the world as it really is.

> A crystal photographs springwater
> as it splashes into natural glass
> so frigid that no furnaces can
> melt it, or so thinks the Sophist
> who decides to drink from alpine
> creeks where he mistakes a flint
> of quartz for ice, only to admire
> that it does not chill his touch
> but despite his warmth defies him.

A crystal is the flashpoint of a dream intense
enough to purge the eye of its infection, sight.

A chance fragment of unblemished quartz
polished in a riverbed by a flowing mixture
of sand and rain may have let Neanderthals
study shadows cast by craters on the moon.

A yardstick inserted into an aquarium
bends in conformity with a localized
curvature of space; however, educated
observers, their senses easily deceived
by evidence of sensory deception, call
this phenomenon an optical illusion.

A word (like love) has a high refractive index.

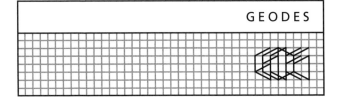

GEODES

GEODES

this antechamber of words
in which you awaken is
a petrified forest, its image
inverted then reflected
through itself, a confusion
of stalactites, stalagmites,
jutting spikes of calcite
at mirrors that do not exist:
a faucet drip, the sound
of outer space underground.

beads of candle wax fall
from silt
icicles, gravity building
the replica
of the ceiling on the floor
over eons
of the most deliberate,
yet unplanned, architecture.

climb across these shelves of rock
in search of this book.

dream of reading through
a passage so narrow
that its walls
threaten
to press into fossils
the broken bones of a breath.

you trip over shadows,
scrape palms on sharp
rocks as small
as glass
from crushed bottles:
their grit clots your wounds.

you follow the distant
murmur of voices in riffling pages.

cracks in the crust of the earth long ago
released hydrogen sulfide,
a gas that percolated up through fissures
in the rocks until it hit
the water table and, reacting with oxygen,
generated sulphuric acid
that ate through the stone and left in its
wake bronchial passages.

be the first to inhale their unbreathed air.

thieves here leave no trace of their
crime, not even the theft of the item.

reset all rocks dislodged underfoot.
brush back into place each cobweb
of thought as you pass through it.
be like the breeze with fireflies in it.

biodegradation is slowed in the cave
so that you are as good as immortal.

all ways are alleyways
that always waylay you.

any path that you take
breaks from its route
in the way that a root
word, when said, gets
tangled in its ganglia.

the secret that you say
sotto voce, like a wish,
ricochets into echoes.

spelunkers find a way
through the cave
by touching on the wall
a textured map
made by the past hands
that have passed over it.

blindfolds
are the logical eyewear.

handholds
are the braille of geology.

arteriosclerotic veins of pyrite
riddle the flesh
of the bedrock (a body drained
of all blood, but refilled
with a golden
transfusion of volcanic magma).

all maps here are axodendritic.

their diagrams
depict the random mutations
of a deformed
anatomy whose disembodied
organs connect without order:

fallopian tubes
act as digestive tracts that join
uterus to anus,
every esophagus an umbilicus
through which bladders evacuate
waste into cul-de-sac stomachs.

you become a castaway adrift
off these islets of langerhans.

this speleological formation imitates
on a grandiose scale
the network of cells
in the fossilized remnants of extinct
porifera that remain
in death absorbative:
the abandoned exoskeleton of a sponge.

the crypt for a googolplex of corpses:

anthozoa, gastropods, crinoids,
bryozoa, brachiopods, blastoids,
echinozoa, scaphopods, cystoids,
archiannelids, entomostracans,
lammelibranchs, cœlenterates.

the lost animalculæ from alien seas.

such dross amassed under the pressure
of its own intensified weight crushes
itself into a sediment for mnemonics.

all the broken letters of the alphabet,
the crustaceous husks of invertebrates.

cascades from subterranean
springs
lacquer slopes
of flowstone into æronautic
contours that nature retests
in wind tunnels.

cloudbursts in brainstorms
osmose through the porous
membranes of these strata,
irrigate this defunct system
of aquifers and aqueducts,
saturate with new meaning
the dead languages of rock.

mudslides cement an onrush
of words into photos of flow.

the smashed bits of clamshells,
molluscs and barnacles stucco
walls with the texture of coral.

you stroll among plough blades
of stone surf,
whose wave crests a stop-action
camera has frozen one instant
before gravity
crashes them down into rubble.

salt frosting
coats baroque rock to create
ice draperies
that unfold into waterfalls,
quartz razors
glittering in a puddle of shards.

an underwater sun of uranium
glows with a chlorinated light
in the coolant of the aquarium.

any bacterium bred in the core
of the reactor evolves over time
into an albino locust that feasts
upon phosphorescent lichen.

pale minnows flit in this cistern
of deuterium, the heavy water
so pure that it cannot conduct
electricity, the surface serene
despite the speed of the current.

a pearl can form in the absence
of any oyster if a bit of salt grit
attains a china finish after being
sprayed by lachrymal splashes.

delicate words simply dissolve
when immersed in their meaning.

deposits of silica crystallize
outward in concentric rings
across the surface of a pond
whose receding water level
leaves behind a bowl of tears
upon a pedestal in a garden:
you steal a drink from this
font, this birdbath for bats.

tiny balloons of magnesite
filled with carbon dioxide
cling like barnacles to a wall
underwater, each a cocoon
for a breath, its fragile shell
releasing, when shattered,
a secret in the drowning cry
of a skindiver – the jellyfish
bubbles floating up to break
open, unheard in the dark.

ripples that lap at the shore
rewrite these marginal notes.

fluorescent algæ on the ceiling can mimic
constellations never seen in the cave.

chemosynthetic bacteria
feed upon sulphur manganese in limestone.
micro-organisms sculpt
crystal growth into bioengineered gardens:

aragonite dandelions,
gypsum bottlebrushes,
rocksalt chandeliers –

hydroponic flowers in plutonic hothouses.

angel-hair crystals, as tall as ten metres,
yet so fragile a breath can destroy them,
twist white vines of frailty into the air,
no wonder expressed for fear of erasing
each wisp of smoke, each vapour trail.

amethyst teeth grow into the yolk
of a geode, each interior crystal
a rock song of thought, an engram
forgotten inside a stone cranium.

follow the path
in the receding mirage of these syllables.

earthquakes low on the richter
scale crack machicolated cliffs:
ramparts, bulwarks, parapets,
collapsing over time into other
variations on the same barricade.

you climb across crenellations
in the form of these sentences:
the buried ruins of battlements
in a fortress sapped by miners –
a toppled panoply of turrets,
cupolas, minarets and steeples.

spiked vocables in these caves
make a phalanx for the pharynx,
their syntax a cheval-de-frise,
a stalactiform portcullis to bar
access to worlds beyond words.

explore this schismatic edifice
through drainpipes and ductwork,
crawl spaces for interconnecting
vaults of nothing but cornices,
all these chambers but clusters
of grapes on the ivy of tunnels.

storm ditches,
ankle-deep in bleached flour,
lead you astray
through catacombs as convoluted
as warrens in an anthill
or canals in the cochlea of an ear.

you step across
the chasms between the words
on these pages,
taking care not to lose footing,
yet you fall into them:
elevator shafts without cables.

a spider rappels down its silk
filament to attack a butterfly
trapped in a cobweb of amber.

landslides
drag you down a funnelled pit
through the waist
of an hourglass
into an oubliette for all sleepers.

gravel showers
bruise your body till you swoon,
the sand a fluid
solid, spilling time away
into dunes on display in tiny jars.

geology writes
a eulogy for all that it buries
by pressing words, like moths,
between pages
of a mammoth encyclopædia.

floating guano dust transforms the reality
of these caverns into a sepia photograph.

stagger through the cave
into a dark planetarium
where, looking up, you see
looking back, a nighttime
sky full of tiny ruby stars,
the eyes of a thousand bats.

vampiric angels who scream in a chorus
castigate you for disturbing their sleep.

the standing ovations
fall from the ceiling
in leathery fragments:

a book with its binding unstitched flung
away at night from the heights of a cliff.

these caverns exhibit avant-garde
sculptures that commemorate
patient, but unknown, architects.

dolomite pagodas, built one grain
of dust at a time, melt in the rain,
like models of mushroom clouds.

obelisks glazed with a glycerol film
of water, as if made from kiln-fired
ceramics, bake in a slow geothermal.

limestone saunas swelter in acidic
vapour, trickles of sweat furrowing
pleats into curtains of sandpaper.

each memory is eroded, not erased,
for the cavern never ceases to record
its history in the code of its crystals.

KEY TO SPELEOLOGICAL FORMATIONS

a – uneroded boulder of dolomite
b – cliffside buttressed by boulder
c – cavern with eroded interior
d – cliffside buttressed by boulder
e – grotto with underhanging ledge
f – waterfall sluicing over precipice
g – eroded obelisk of flowstone
h – cliffside with abutting archway
i – plinth from broken stalagmite
j – precipice with collapsed ledge
k – cliffside with flying buttresses
l – unbroken column of dolomite
m – cavernous vault of stalactites
n – archway of oolitic limestone
o – weathered boulder of dolomite

p – precipice with overhanging grotto
q – precipice with overhanging grotto
r – overhanging shelf of bedrock
s – escarpment with avalanching scree
t – crumbling column with ledges
u – trench from alluvial riverbed
v – geological fissure cut in bedrock
w – cavernous field of stalagmites
x – reputed location of buried treasure
y – cleft with underhanging ledge
z – escarpment with overhanging ledge
- – sandstone bridge over canyon
, – rock fragment containing fossils
. – rock fragment containing geodes
: – exposed seam of precious minerals

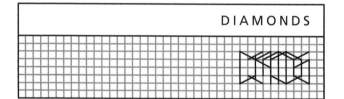

DIAMONDS

DIAMONDS

1

C IS FOR DIAMOND

THE ONE GEM

MADE OF ONE

ELEMENT: CARBON

CHIMNEY SOOT
CRUSHED COAL
CHARRED WOOD

FIRE AT ITS CORE

MY FATHER   HE MADE JEWELS MORE PRECIOUS
WAS A SAD   BY SMASHING THEM, SPOKE ONLY
GEMCUTTER   WORDS PARED DOWN TO THE EDGE
                   OF THEIR SILENCE, AND STROVE

                   TO BREAK INTO (BREAK OUT OF)

                        EACH HOUSE
                        OF MIRRORS

                   HELD AT THE TIP OF HIS TONGS

MY FATHER   HE RETIRED, NERVES
TAUGHT ME   SHOT BY THE THREAT
PRECISION   OF A SLIPPED RAZOR

2

A DIAMOND IS   TRANSPARENT CHARCOAL:

A DARKNESS   UNDER PRESSURE
SO INTENSE   ALL THINGS ARE
                                CLEAR, BUT JUST
THE EYE SEES
                                BE SURE TO REMEMBER:
THROUGH IT   DIAMOND DUST IS BLACK

MY FATHER ONCE
GAVE ME A GIFT

AN APACHE TEAR
A BLACK PEBBLE

                                THEN THE SMOKE
OPAQUE UNTIL I HELD IT   TRAPPED INSIDE
UP AGAINST DIRECT LIGHT   BECAME VISIBLE

AFTER HOURS OF SOLITUDE   THE NATIVE WIDOW
WHEN DRUNK, HE RECALLED   WHO LAMENTED HER
                                LOSS FOR SO LONG
                                THE GREAT SPIRIT
                                TRANSFIGURED HER
                                TEARS INTO DROPS
                                OF BLACK CRYSTAL
                                THUS BEQUEATHING

                                TO ALL WHO FALL IN LOVE
                                KEEPSAKES OF HER SORROW

MY FATHER
TOO BROKE
TO BE WED
NEVER GOT   HE CLAIMED TO ADORE HER
MY MOTHER   TOO MUCH TO PROFANE HER
A DIAMOND   WITH GEMS MADE OF ASHES

3

BLOWTORCH A DIAMOND

ENKINDLED
WHEN RUBY
IT BLAZES

JUST AS
MELTING DRY ICE

VAPORIZES AS A BREATH

ORGANIC STONE

NOT STERILE
BUT BURNING

CRYSTALS MADE

FROM THE SAME

THING AS LIFE

LIFE: THE PERCENTAGE OF LIGHT THAT A DIAMOND
REFLECTS BACK TOWARDS ITS VIEWER

FIRE: THE DEGREE TO WHICH A DIAMOND REFRACTS
LIGHT INTO ITS COMPONENT COLOURS

A B C D E F G H I J K L M N O P Q R S T U V W X Y Z

MY FATHER OPENED THE FIELD
GUIDE TO CRYSTALS TO PAGES
WITH FINE PRINT TO SHOW ME
HOW TO DECIPHER A LANGUAGE

HE GAVE ME HIS GEMCUTTER'S
EYEPIECE AND LEFT ME ALONE
TO REVEL IN DETAIL: EDGES
OF SERIFS, FIBRES IN PAPER

ONLY LATER DID HE TEACH ME
HOW TO SOUND OUT THE WORDS

LIFE × FIRE = BRILLIANCE: (ALL THIS IS TRUE)

4

PLATO WAS
THE FIRST
TO REGARD

A DIAMOND AS
FROZEN QUINTESSENCE

A SOUL IN
SUSPENDED
ANIMATION

A VESTIGE OF HEAVEN
WITHIN EARTH

MY FATHER
TAUGHT ME
PRECISION

HE STUDIED   TENDED SAW   SAW
MINERALOGY   FOR A FIRM   ONE
AT ANTWERP   IN BRÜCKEN   GEM

                                                  TAKE TWO
                                                  YEARS TO
                                                  BE SPLIT
                                                  INTO TWO

                                                  DEI MUNDI

ALL HIS LIFE AN ATTEMPT   MY FATHER
TO SEE THE FREE POINT   PUT FAITH
TRAPPED IN PERFECTION   IN NO GOD

5

A MEMBER OF THE CUBIC   PLATONIC SOLIDS
CRYSTAL SYSTEM

A DIAMOND DENOTES   NATURE NEEDS
THE HIGHEST   NO TOOL
STATE OF SYMMETRY   AND DIE
                               TO MAKE

AN IDEAL ARRAY
OF CUTS, ACUTE ANGLES   ITS OCTAHEDRONS

                                    D
                CRYSTAL: I   N
                S(HARD)S   A   M   O
                                I   N
                                    D

A DIAMOND IS AN EQUILATERAL TRIANGLE
THAT MIRRORS ITSELF THROUGH ONE SIDE

OVER DRINKS AFTER HOURS
OF STRESS OVER DIAMONDS
AN EXPERT IN THE MAKING
OF FAKE GEMS BET NO ONE
WAS ABLE TO TELL OF TWO
GEMS WHICH WAS THE TRUE
ONE, WHICH WAS THE COPY

WITHOUT
USE OF EITHER
SCRATCH
PLATE OR LENS

NO JEWELLER
WON THE BET
BUT THE ONE

WHO LET
THE TWO

GEMS
DROP
INTO

HIS CRÈME
DE MENTHE

THE ONE THAT SANK
SLOWER WAS A FAKE

6

ADAMAS MEANS INVINCIBLE

NO KNOWN JEWEL
IN THE MINERAL KINGDOM
RIVALS DIAMOND

KING OF STONES
ADAMANT IN THE SILENCE
NO WORDS BREAK

IN(DI)VISIBLE AS A STAR

ONLY DIAMONDS
SCAR DIAMONDS

SAWYERS THOUGHT
MY FATHER CRAZY

THE   HIS   WAS
DAY   EYE   CUT

OPEN BY A STRAY
CHIP OF DIAMOND

HIS MIND MAKING
HIS HAND FINISH

ITS ADJUSTMENTS
TO THE SAW BLADE

BEFORE BREAKING
OUT IN A SCREAM

AFTERWARDS
HIS REGRET

HIS SIGHT WAS SAVED
BUT NOT THE DIAMOND

7

MAZARIN, RONDELLE, PERUZZI

A DIAMOND'S
CUT IS JUST

TRILLIANT
PENDELOQUE
BRIOLETTE

A JEWELLER'S

PRETTY NAME

CHIFFRE, MARQUISE, JUBILEE

FOR A WOUND

MY FATHER NEVER
BREATHING A LIE
BRILLIANTEERING

DESIGNED TABLES
UPON WHICH ONLY
THE EYE FEASTED

FASHIONED GIRDLES
AND CULETS TO FIT
IMPERVIOUS ARMOUR

ERECTED PAVILIONS
ABOVE WHICH KITES
AND STARS HOVERED

THE BRUTED
GEM SET IN
ITS DOP IS
SCOURED BY
THE SCAIFE
A GRINDING
DISK OILED
WITH A MIX
OF DIAMOND
POWDER AND
LUBRICANTS

A LAPIDARY
GRAMOPHONE

ITS STYLUS
WEARS AWAY
ITS SONG
EVEN AS IT
SINGS IT

THE MEREST
HAMMERBLOW
ON A BLADE
WHOSE EDGE
CUTS ALONG
A KERF CAN
SHEAR AWAY
THE FAULTS
OF ANY GEM

ADAMANTINE
DISCIPLINE

INFLEXIBLE
EXACTITUDE

MY SHOCK
AT BLOOD

WHERE HE NICKED
A CHEEK SHAVING

8

TRANSPARENCY
IS THE GAUGE
OF ALL VALUE
WHEN CUTTING
WHEN WRITING

A DIAMOND IS
AN ABSENCE
OF NOTHING
BUT DARKNESS

OCCLUSIONS
SUPPOSEDLY
DEPRECIATE
PERFECTION

~~OCCLUSIONS~~
~~PERFECTION~~

MY FATHER SPOTTED FLAWS
BY BREATHING ON A STONE

TO DULL THE LUSTRE
THAT OBSCURED THEM

BUBBLES
FEZELS
CRACKS
NAATS
CLOUDS
GLATTS
FRINGES

CARBON STRAINS
TO CREATE LIFE

HE SHOWED ME A DIAMOND
WHOSE DEFECT RESEMBLED
A DIMINUTIVE BUTTERFLY

IN THE IMAGE
OF ITS FLAWS

9

DIAMOND IS FORMED BY DETONATING   ·   DIAMOND:
GRAPHITE IN A COMPACT CONTAINER

FLAT BLACK

GRAPHITE

BENT CLEAR

[CRYSTALLIZED CARBON
GRAPHITE AND DIAMOND
HAVE NEARLY THE SAME

ATOMIC: (BLACK ICE)
MATRIX: (A LATTICE)   [SWEET SPACES
BETWEEN WORDS
A COLD JIGSAW PUZZLE   BETWEEN ATOMS
ITS PIECES HEXAGONS   IN AMONG THEM
ABANDONED HONEYCOMB]   STRONG BONDS]

MY FATHER DETESTED   A BLUNT INSTRUMENT
WRITING   BY WHICH HE DULLED
                             EDGES OF PENKNIVES
WITH A DULL PENCIL   (MY OWN KNIVES) TO
                             SHARPEN THE POINTS
WRITING   MADE IN HIS MANUAL
TO HIM MEANT USING   ON DIAMOND-CUTTING

MY FATHER ONCE STOLE A DIAMOND DISCARDED
AS WORTHLESS AT WORK AND USING CORROSIVE
AND SAWBLADE ETCHED INTO IT HIS MONOGRAM
AS THOUGH TO BE RID OF A SCAR BY LEAVING
BEHIND HIM A SCAR, A NAME TO OUTLAST HIM

MEDIEVAL ARABS NEEDED NO LASERS TO CARVE
THEIR PRAYERS ONTO THE FACES OF DIAMONDS

10

A SHAH CAPTURED IN WAR REFUSED TO SURRENDER
THE LOCATION OF THE KOH-I-NUR, THE MOUNTAIN
OF LIGHT, EVEN THOUGH TORTURERS BLINDED HIM

A DUKE WHO NEVER LET HIS GEMSTONES BE TAKEN
FROM HIS SIGHT FOR FEAR OF LOSING THEM LOST
THE FLORENTINE WHILE IN BATTLE, THE DIAMOND
FOR DAYS AMID WEEDS THEN MISTAKEN FOR GLASS
BY A GUARD WHO SOLD IT TO A MONK FOR A FLORIN

AVOIRDUPOIS   MY FATHER
TROY OUNCES   APPRAISED
                                     THE VALUE
THE SLIGHT WEIGHT   IN CARATS
OF ONE CAROB SEED   FOR A GEM
CAN TIP A FRAGILE
BALANCE OF FORCES   WITH THE USE OF NO
IN A COMMONWEALTH   SCALE BUT HIS HAND

THE ORLOFF WAS STOLEN FROM THE EYE
OF A GOD BY A SOLDIER IN THE GUISE
OF A PRIEST SO THAT LATER A PRINCE
MIGHT TRY IN VAIN TO WOO A CZARINA

A SULTAN ONCE WORSHIPPED THE MATAN
BECAUSE OF THE DEMONS LOCKED IN IT
SAFEGUARDING THE LAW OF HIS EMPIRE

MY FATHER TRUSTING
NO FICTION BECAUSE

IT TOLD LIES
TOLD ME ONLY
TRUE STORIES

ABOUT THE EXPLOITS
OF MEN OWNING GEMS

A WEALTHY COLLECTOR
JEALOUS OF A FUTURE
POSSESSOR COMMANDED
SERVANTS TO SHATTER
THE PIGOT, ITS BITS
IN HIS GRIP CUTTING
HIM AS HE LAY DYING

THE HOPE WAS A CURSE

11

CULLINAN   VIOLENT WORDS UNDER MINING
EXCELSIOR
LESOTHO   SLAVES EXCAVATE
COROMANDEL   RAW ICE
BERGLEN   OUT OF THE BLUE
KIMBERLEY
VICTORIA   TOPSOIL
                           FROM AN EXTINCT
                           VOLCANO

IMPERIAL
DIAMONDS   WARM KIMBERLITE
SUNDERED   ITS ASH
TO ADORN   A STARRY MEADOW
WEDDINGS
AND WARS   YIELDS DIMINISH WITH DEPTH

AD DOMINAM OMNIS

GEMS DOT A SKY
WITH THEIR OWN
CONSTELLATIONS

A HANDFUL
OF STONES
FLUNG MOONWARD

A PROMISE
TO SUMMON
METEOR SHOWERS

EVERY VOW
A NET SET
TO CATCH STARS

EVERY LIE
A RIP CUT
IN THE THREADS

WE FUMBLE
FOR WORDS
AMIDST CINDERS

WE BARTER
WITH BITS
OF BRIGHT HAIL

12

SIR ISAAC NEWTON
IN THEORY
DEFINED DIAMOND
AS AN 'UNCTUOUS
SUBSTANCE
MUCH COAGULATED'

THE BLOOD
OF ANGELS
CONGEALED
INTO HARD
TEARDROPS
OF PURITY

THE PHYSICIST EVEN HAD
A DOG NAMED DIAMOND

THE GIRL'S BEST FRIEND
WAS ALSO ONCE A MAN'S

LONG DIVISION
AMONG SAWYERS

WORD
$= 23 + 15 + 18 + 4$
$= 60$
$= 4 + 9 + 1 + 13 + 15 + 14 + 4$
$=$ DIAMOND

THE REDUCTION
OF ONE
TO
TWO TO
MAKE MILLIONS

MY FATHER BECOMING   CRYSTAL
THE GIFTED PROTEGÉ   CLASSES
DESPITE POOR BIRTH
                                      ORGANIC
DISCOVERED   UNDERSTOOD   UNITIES
ARITHMETIC   PERFECTION
BY READING   BY SOLVING   MAGICAL
TRIG TEXTS   ON HIS OWN   SQUARES
WHEN SEVEN   WHEN EIGHT

THE TRANSCENDENTAL   101   5   71
CORRELATION PROVEN   29   59   89
BY EULER'S THEOREM   47   113   17

$$e^{i\pi} + 1 = 0$$

MY FATHER   ALWAYS TRYING TO MAKE HIS
TAUGHT ME   MIND FIT THE MATHEMATICAL
PRECISION   STRAITJACKET OF A JEWEL

13

DIAMOND HAS A HIGH
THERMOCONDUCTIVITY

CRYSTAL FILMS
MINIATURIZING
COMMUNICATION

ABSORBING HEAT
FASTER
THAN ANY OTHER
MATTER
KNOWN TO EXIST

A PRECIOUS COATING
TO COOL MICROCHIPS

MY FATHER
THE MODEL
OF POETIC
RESTRAINT

EVERY JEWEL A FIST
WHICH STRAINS
TO KEEP HARSH LIGHT
FROM SPILLING
THROUGH ITS FINGERS

THE TONE OF HIS
VOICE UNCHANGED
EVEN WHEN ANGRY

MY FATHER   MORE LIFE MEANS
COULD NOT   LESS FIRE, MORE
FORMULATE   FIRE MEANS LESS
THE WORDS   LIFE: HE FOUND
TO CREATE   A WAY TO STRIKE
OUT OF US

                                              A DIAMOND
ONE MACLE   TO STRIKE
A TWINNED   A BALANCE
GEMSTONE

                                         BETWEEN THE TWO
HE DEEMED
ME A NAIF
A NATURAL
FACET YET   I
TO BE CUT   A M
                                          I   N
THE BLADE OF SILENCE BETWEEN US   A
                                         D I   M
THE UNSPOKEN BURNING INSIDE HIM   D I A M O N D

14

APRIL BIRTHSTONE
REVERENT FOREVER

MEDICAL REMEDIES
IN ANCIENT TIMES
CLAIMED DIAMONDS
NULLIFIED POISON

STEEL INDUSTRIES
USE DIAMOND BORT
AS ABRASIVE GRIT
IN IRON GRINDING

ARABIAN ASSASSINS
MIXED INTO WATER
POWDERED DIAMOND
TO EXECUTE KINGS

THE RED COUGHING
OF MY SAD FATHER
SIPPING HIS LAST
SHOTS OF LIQUEUR
LACED WITH GLASS
TRYING TO ESCAPE
THE VERY DIAMOND
CRUSHED INTO HOT
ASHES INSIDE HIM

I AM, AND I
AM, AND
I AM, AND I
AM, AND
I DIE, AMEN

MY FATHER
UNTO DEATH
TAUGHT ME
THE DIVINE
ENDURANCE
OF DIAMOND

A DAMNED DIAMOND
FOR A MAD DOMAIN

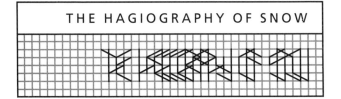

THE HAGIOGRAPHY OF SNOW

CRYSTALS

A crystal may take as long to grow as a star at the edge
of the universe may take to show its presence in the sky.

                        A crystal manufactures itself tier
                                by tier, each epitaxial layer
                                so thin that crystallization
                        is akin to a pharaoh, whose slaves
                                build for him a pyramid
                                by applying infinite coats
                        of paint to the same surface area.

A crystal is a mineral blossom, never quick to germinate
in pure solutions since the flower needs a flaw to form
a substrate for its calyx.

                        A crystal is the most exquisite
                        parasite upon a spindrift seed.

                        A white pearl goes slowly nova
                        from a particle of black sand.

A tulip dipped in liquid
nitrogen undergoes instantaneous cryonics, whereupon
the flower can be smashed to bits as easily as a wineglass.

A word when read aloud is such a crystal being (being)
shattered by a sequence of high-frequency vibrations.

SNOWFLAKES

OPAL

```
        H
S       Y
I   H Y D R O G E N
L       R
I   O   O X Y G E N
C   X   G
O X Y G E N
N   G   N
    E
    N
```

ombré silverbirches

organza
obscure

harlequin hailstorm

KALOKAGATHIA

stars are bubbles of air

rising through an infinite

depth: we rise with them

through this dark, slow

motion snowfall in reverse

sleep through our ascent

bound at wrist and ankle

by the chains from silver

watches, anchors without

weight: even as we dream

we hold our breath against

the moment when we crash

up through the surface

tension, as though through

a sheet of glass, into still

another depth with other

stars, the fragments of our

last collision in our wake

eyes shut tight, and every

mouth a photo of a scream

FIGURE 1.0: A goniometric device for measuring
the interfacial angles of a crystal

Turbulent winds can break off the fragile branches of a stellar
crystal as it falls, and often the branches regenerate during the
descent, but even after reaching the ground these fragments
can suffer further modification: winds can disintegrate each
crystal by abrading it against other crystals so that, when the
fallen remnant comes to rest at last beneath the microscope
of the observer, the specimen often bears little resemblance
to the original particle formed high in the ionosphere.

[TRIPTYCH]

dark glass by the bed at night
three paintings in pale stains

love

a triptych of frost fractals

white
        ferns awash
in moonglare
   leaves
      serrated
clash, cross swords
   feather
      edges bristle
into each other

three cobweb arabesques

look

through each pane at winter
yet not so close lest words

be trapped

in the icy latticework of breath

frost developing its nocturnal film
reveals neural maps on windows

love

is the intricate growth of a crystal
in a dream of time-lapse photography

each moment
dendritic

a juncture
that branches

out into
all of its

possible
foliage

each decision a routine for pruning
the tree, itself a curtain of razors

look

at each screen of crystalliferous scars
beyond which a sky of eiderdown falls

the white arborescence of flame
beheld in the flash of a stroboscope

love

lets you contemplate its negative
at the instant in which it is taken

foil
mirror
backs

lace
bridal
veils

rice
paper
fans

all nothing more than mere
smoke embroidered in these windows

look

beyond the translucence of writing
to a cryonic kiss before sleep

TRIGON MIRROR

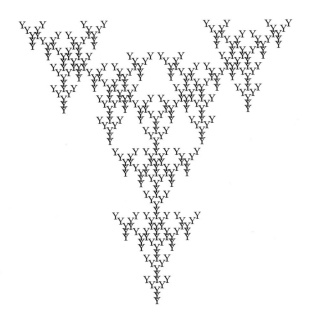

FIGURE 1.1: A photomicrograph of the letter Y magnified
25× to reveal its innate crystalline structure

Chandelier breezes at midnight, actinic, wash over a back-drop of linen, upon which transparency machines make bioluminescent the image of snow. Nightfall meadows seen through screen doors at wintertime undulate into felsen-meers strobe-lit like a slow-mo chiaroscuro. Mammals, hibernating, simultaneously twitch in their cryogenic sleep, each a seasonal fœtus in its bleach amnion. Vodka drips from the tip of an icicle. Neon moonlight amplifies this field of vision beyond whose horizons all events vanish.

Deciduous trees, black without foliation, etch neural pathways on a dream of glass photographs. Nitrates of silver electroplate mirrors. Peroxide evaporates from smashed ampoules of ice. Timberwolves circle the clearing. Two pan-tomime children perform there the drama of winter. The girl in lace pouring pitchers of ice water over the kneeling form of her nude sister, whose shivers subside into an icy chrysalis. The audience unseen as it watches liquid nitrogen spill over the edge of the stage.

Ethereal theatre.

December constellations in vacuum-tube skies glitter until smashed by a breath into blizzards. Microscopic, the shrapnel from distant explosions administers a cold acu-puncture. Quartz grit dancing in the fray of highbeam glare. Miniscule pinwheels, bladed, cut into the windshield. Silent attack without witness, the driver drifting to sleep at the wheel as he breathes in time to slow jazz intermixed with soft radio static. Astronavigation through a snow squall. Pulverized mirrors, whose reflections, broken, make us dream that the darkness assails us with stars.

Nacreous confetti.

Snowdrifts avalanche at the hush of a hammer and feather dropped by an astronaut upon lunar ashes. Birch trees in moonlight cast zebra shadows. Mercury streams decant themselves over rock gardens, cool acid dissolving the myelin frost. Snowy owls never take wing, but use astral projection to glide into the violence of prey. Hypoxic, every breath in the rarefied air. Nerves ionized to the point of pinprick electrocution. Frozen, the cobwebs obscure the view through this window.

Peppermint daylight at noon upon firnspiegel burns like a magnesium flare, each grain of ice a tiny heliograph that flashes a telepathic transmission. Waterford crystal juts its stalactites down from the eaves. Damoclean, the swords glint in a row, the heat from your body beneath triggering the fall. Narwhal horns. Viking boys snap off bayonets from crystalline arsenals so as to stab each other to death, their weapons diluting the blood of their wounds. Sunshine oils hockey rinks with a frictionless skiff of cool water.

Diamantiferous fields of white alluvia. Wind chimes of glass dangle from wire fences. Draft-borne argosies of snow. Frozen dust motes accrete on the tips of eyelashes. Iridium skies toned at the horizon with pewter. Airless desolation. Lead poisoning from solder in tin cans of food drives Arctic explorers so insane that they scuttle their old ships to board new ships seen in melting icebergs. Barns in the pale haze, the grey hulls of battleships run aground among ice floes. Words stumbling in the shrill blank of snow blindness. Deer hoof-prints in plaster. Ski tracks, like railways for phantom trolley cars passing through the night without passengers.

Aurora borealis.

Moonlight on graupel, the cool, silvery gleam of galena crystals embedded in radio rectifiers. Dandelion seeds of frost descend through the beam of a searchlight onto languid rivers of India ink, each snowflake an ephemeral microcircuit beneath the lens of a magnifying glass. Waterfalls spotlit at the border. Cascades unfurling into bridal stage-curtains for concealing escarpments of thunder. Evanescent, the mist from the chasm, ossifying into a thick calcification on handrails and streetlamps. Alabaster sculptures that thought conjures from thin air.

Christmas mirages.

Snowploughs, unmanned, patrol empty streets bathed in a sapphire penumbra. Somnambulistic machines. Lacteal surf in the wake of their bulldozer blades flows over the bodies of etherized lovers. Cocaine spindrift whirls away across barren parking lots. Seismic tremors on a moonscape agitate soap dust inside the glass paperweight. Pale sparks filmed for a silent movie shower down from a sheet of black steel being cut by an arc welder. Wind in midwinter is an X-ray that opens as a portal before you.

White canopies of felt slip from their hooks on pine branches. Arctic voles riddle with tunnels the subnivean layer just as insects etch wormholes beneath the bark of a dead tree. Feathery rime on a timberline snag. Icicle stemware. Invisible, the silversmiths laminate limestone with platinum alloy. Northern lakes protect their exposed surfaces with acrylic membranes. Glycerol pools beneath cedars. Algæ fronds sway beneath the windowpane of a pond. Skywriting preserved in the wake of your skateblades. Ice is a solid acid that eats into water. We figure eight to infinity.

Stranded archæologists dine on prehistoric meat from a woolly mammoth paralyzed for ten millennia inside a receding glacier. Chalk dust settles over tamaracks. Chalets in the valley leak genies of blue smoke from their chimneys at night. Albinic, the blind men ski down wooded slopes to feed on the nightmares of children. Glaze, a seminal translucence on the snowpack at dawn, each footstep punching through a thin pane, jagged edges that make a bear trap for the ankle. Words sinter together in a subzero network of delicate needles, the most fragile of structures because it collapses into itself at the merest disturbance. Angel-dust névé stirred into cirrus clouds by the wraiths in their passing.

Suspended animation.

Tuning forks shatter this architecture by means of sympathetic resonance. Supercooled droplets of sleet prickle the steel hood of a crashed car. Xylophonic tintinnabulation. Tambourine hail. Glass bits from the windshield salt the street. Pine trees, pointillistic with ginger fireflies, tungsten bulbs that flicker too fast for the eye. Polar bears maul garbage cans in the alley. Slush on the sidewalk insulates the cellophane wrapper that blooms into a diaphanous flower.

Pearlescent sunlight.

Toboggans smouldering in the remains of a bonfire at the bottom of the ravine, but no bodies. Sentences such as these broadcast events at dusk in the grey monochrome of television. Ermine, the niveous pelage. Ivory pagodas with skeletons of blue spruce barricade the forest. Stiff bristles of aragonite fill cracks in the wall of the hibernarium. Lavender skies and pink lights of a city in the distance.

Excelsior twilight.

Harpsichord wind through the trees. Moonrise with its paraselene gives every silhouette an argent corona. Private concert in the gazebo, where a girl rubs her moist fingers round the rims of brandy glasses half-filled with distilled water. Sonatinas so pure that their music seems to originate elsewhere. Winter transforms the world into a jewellery store, where Lalique crystal gleams on mirrored shelves in the dark. Snow upon your lips has the taste of chrome sugar.

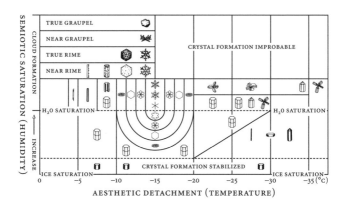

FIGURE 1.2: A graph charting the meteorological conditions
necessary for the crystallization of poetic forms

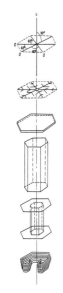

Semiotic saturation increases from a solid state of monosemy to a fluid state of polysemy until meaning etherealizes itself in the region of cloud formation. Solid columns (CLE) in the region of stabilization signify the restricted economy of grammatical referentiality, since such crystals maintain a low state of semiotic saturation across the entire continuum of æsthetic detachment. Poetry lies in zones of disequilibrium.

Temperatures above −10°C correspond approximately to romantic versification, with scrolled columns (CLI) designating, for example, the anamnestic analecta by both William Wordsworth and Samuel Taylor Coleridge. Temperatures between −10°C and −20°C correspond approximately to modernist experimentation, with stellar dendrites (PLE) designating, for example, the anagogical analecta by both T. S. Eliot and Ezra Pound. Temperatures below −20°C correspond approximately to postmodernist instrumentation, with crystal aggregates (S3) designating, for example, the anagrammatic analecta by both Steve McCaffery and bpNichol.

Poetry that is rimed is often very prolix, but not very cool. Blank sectors refer to regions in which poetic composition is virtually impossible, since poetry that is very cool can only reach a certain limit of semiotic saturation before it must resort to rime and thereby forsake some of its coolness. Graupel refers to the infinite semiosis of eloquent silence, the transcendental nature of which is currently unfashionable.

FIGURE 1.2 situates itself on the chart within the vicinity of crystal S3. Consult THE CRYOMETRIC INDEX OF POETIC FORMS for more information.

		RHYMED	METRED	REFERENTIAL	GRAMMATICAL	PHONIC	ICONIC	POLYSEMIC	ASEMANTIC	ELEGIAC	SATIRIC
	NLA ELEMENTARY NEEDLE		•			•	•				
	NLC ELEMENTARY SHEATH		•			•	•				
	NLE COLUMNAR NEEDLE		•		•	•	•				
	CLC SOLID BULLET				•	•	•				•
	CLD HOLLOW BULLET					•	•				•
	CLE SOLID COLUMN				•	•	•				
	CLF HOLLOW COLUMN					•	•				
	CLG SOLID PLATE				•			•			
	CLF HOLLOW PLATE							•		•	
	CLI SCROLL				•		•			•	
	C2A BULLET COMBINATION					•	•		•		•
	PLA HEXAGONAL PLATE				•			•			
	PLB SECTORED PLATE		•		•			•	•		
	PLC BRANCHED PLATE		•		•			•			
	PLD STELLAR CRYSTAL		•			•	•		•		
	PLE DENDRITIC CRYSTAL		•			•	•		•	•	
	PLF PTERIDEOUS CRYSTAL		•			•	•		•	•	
	S1 PLANAR AGGREGATE				•		•	•	•	•	
	S2 COLUMNAR CLUSTER				•	•	•	•	•	•	•
	RLA FROSTED NEEDLE	•	•			•	•				
	RLB FROSTED COLUMN	•				•	•				
	RLC FROSTED PLATE	•			•			•			
	RLD FROSTED DENDRITE	•	•			•	•		•		
	R2A RIMED PLATE	•			•			•			
	R2B RIMED DENDRITE	•	•			•	•		•	•	
	R3A AGGREGATE GRAUPEL	•					•		•	•	
	R3B HEXAGONAL GRAUPEL										

THE CRYOMETRIC INDEX OF POETIC FORMS

EUCLID AND HIS MODERN RIVALS

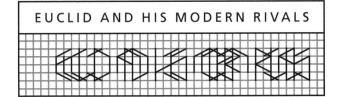

RENÉ JUST-HAÜY (1743–1822)

Repetition of the same name, & the same name, & the same
name, & the same name, benumbs us to its sum of meaning.

Crystals partition space with intersecting arrays of parallel
lines, and these lines, when woven together, form a complex
lattice of letters, used to build trellises for the ivy of thought.

Icelandic spar, despite its outward form, cracks
apart along its fracture planes into rhombohedra,
as if these words, when parsed, reveal themselves
to be composed of one letter constantly repeated.

A fractal crumbles into a smaller copy of its unbroken state.

Stars die in a DISASTER
that SHATTERS the stars.

Cubes of salt contain
mineral holograms.

They reveal a complicity between complexity and simplicity.

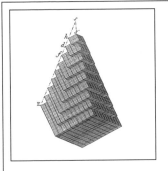

A botanist dropping calcite shards beholds them break into regular patterns, every piece a tiny brick of glass for building, stack by stack, apartment blocks of prison houses – riot cells for souls.

FIGURE 2.0: The polysyndeton of crystal polyhedrons

Lattices form crossword puzzles, diagramless and unsolvable.

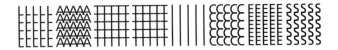

Language acts like a wire grid in a window of reinforced glass.

Crystallographers who map the myriad facets of a jewel must
learn to see the outside of the earth upon the inside of the sky.

Crystals are atlases of nothingness,
the world disappearing but leaving
behind its latitudes and longitudes.

The map must never let its readers
see the jewel itself, but must show
them how to reconstruct it into view.

Dewey decimal numbers triangulate the position of a cubic
facet, like the cover of a book, in a stacked archive of surfaces.

Planes are
mere plans
for panels
and panes.

The name of a newfound star begins with an alphanumeral,
the letter A denoting the most brilliant or most proximate.

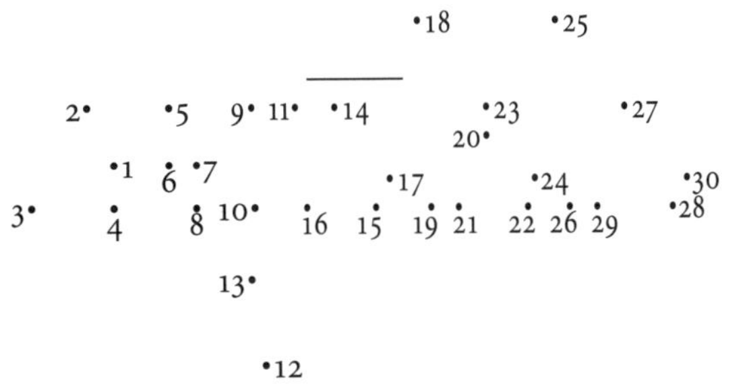

FIGURE 2.1: The constellation of stellar coordinates

Crystallographers play connect-the-dots with these galaxies
of thought colliding in the cloud chambers of a darkroom.

The last three letters of the alphabet
christen every single point in space.

Properties of the crystalline are proper ties for the crystal line.

AUGUSTE BRAVAIS (1811–1863)

Crystals maintain the integrity of their structure by forcing
each of their parts to tear the whole away from all other parts.

Lattices map a stable configuration of lines
within a closed system of semiotic relations,
every vertex a node of tension, suspended
like a letter among syllables, inside the fields
of force emanating from every other vertex.

Geometry proves that only fourteen varieties of stalemate
can occur during the endgames for such atomic tug-of-wars.

Crystals are acrostics generated by the stochastics of a cage.

Lattices gridlock
bits of symmetry
inside networks
of microcircuitry.

Lattices distribute points throughout a space in the same way
that a spondee or a trochee distributes stress across a line.

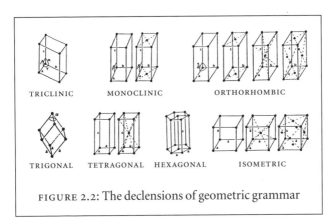

FIGURE 2.2: The declensions of geometric grammar

```
A T O M    C U B E    W O R D    U N I T    Z O N E
T Y P E    U P O N    O B O E    N O D E    O K A Y
O P A L    B O L D    R O S E    I D E A    N A M E
M E L T    E N D S    D E E P    T E A R    E Y E S
```

Tinkertoys permit children at play to learn through intuition
the grammatical fundamentals of a crystalline architecture.

FRIEDRICH MOHS (1773–1839)

Pretty words, like *fluorite* or *feldspar,* are far too soft for sale
as gemstones, since they suffer wear when worn as jewellery.

Words can chip away at each other when jostled together.

```
Wor s      hip    a  t eac    her when     led to    her.
W r        i         t e      her w  e     l d        er.
W          i         t        h    e                   r.
W          i         t
           i         t
           i
```

Writing represents the superficial damage endured by one
surface when inflicting damage upon the surface of another.

Angels reside inside
the angles of galena.

The Neoplatonic universe is a glass onion, in which each layer
swivels around a rotten core, the worm-eaten cosmos a mere
chrysalis for a god, doomed to climb heavenward on a ladder
of finite rungs by transferring the bottom rungs to the top.

0	DIAMOND	ELOHIM
9	CORUNDUM	SERAPHIM
8	TOPAZ	OPHANIM
7	QUARTZ	CHERUBIM
6	ORTHOCLASE	SHINNANIM
5	APATITE	TARSHISHIM
4	FLUORITE	HASHMALLIM
3	CALCITE	MALAKIM
2	GYPSUM	ARELIM
1	TALC	ZILIM

Each mineral abraded
by all minerals above it
can abrade only itself
& all minerals below it.

FIGURE 2.3: The celestial hierarchy of mineralogy

The Great Chain of Being
is now deoxyribonucleic.

A chromosome can encode its genes within the sequence   .
of its crystals, every codon like a bead upon a spiral abacus.

SOFT ⟶ SORT ⟶ SORE ⟶ CORE ⟶ CORD ⟶ CARD ⟶ HARD

L. A. NECKER (1786–1861)

Cubes incubate ambiguity about the rubric of their structure.

Unable to register both meanings of a homonym at the same
time, the mind in its indecision must vacillate between two
possible, but contrary, interpretations of the same message.

The cube emulates the form of a photon,
a phenomenon existing two ways at once:
both mote and wave – a quantum pun,
in which the universe must take delight.

The homonyms that generate poetic interference split in two
when passing through the double-slit experiments of speech.

LIGHT IS NOT HEAVY

English models content to play
with the lead of the cast type in this script.

A man with an appetite for apatite
puts quarts of quartz into barrels of beryls.

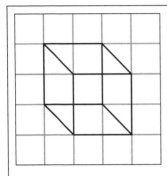

The cube exists in two dimensions at the same time, while appearing to shift at random back and forth between them without ever seeming to occupy both at once.

FIGURE 2.4: The optical paronomasia of crystallography

The two words 'two words'
are either 'either' and 'or'
or both 'both' and 'and'
unless one of the words
is two 'words' or one 'two.'

The word at the end of this sentence is meaningless.

MAX VON LAUE (1879-1960)

X-ray machines that bombard the lattice of a crystal turn
its skeleton and its scaffold into shadows cast by tesseracts.

Mondrian drafted blueprints
for a set of integrated circuits,
linking lines in zones of colour.

Mondrian painted microchips,
each magnified a millionfold,
but died before patenting them.

When we study radiograms, we learn how to understand
a poem by reading nothing but its pattern of punctuation.

Cosmic rays make salt fluoresce
in day-glo green and hot-wax
lemon (colours in the spectrum
of phosphorus and kryptonite),
even a blue, like backlit curaçao.

Each crystal is an optic sieve for the lightshows that suffuse it.

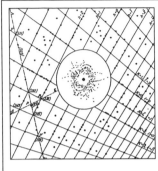

X-rays emit at wavelengths
short enough to fit between
the bars of an atomic cage,
all its walls electric fences,
all its cells black boxes lit
by a burst of invisible light.

FIGURE 2.5: The gnomonic projection of textuality

Writing is an obsolete machine
for CAT scanning drops of frost
caught within a web of dreams.

The gossamer ghost of a skull gazes at us from black celluloid.

Viruses are crystals come to life when exposed to radiation.

W. L. BRAGG (1890–1971)

X-rays illuminate black bodies with a light that no one sees,
the sound of its flicker preserved in the shape of its silence.

The loops and whorls of fingerprints
resemble magnetic fields
emanating from electrons
in a crystal of amino acid
whose genes go on to yield
the loops and whorls of fingerprints.

Each of us emits an infrared aura as unique as any signature.

Sand can dance into a pattern on the skin of a vibrant drum.

A crystal contains immobile
cyclones in its vacuum tubes.

Isograms for storm fronts propagate in waves across the page.

Stellar clusters seen on the video screen of a radio telescope
reveal the crystal lattices that support a microscopic cosmos.

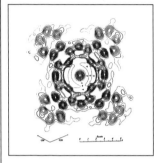

X-ray machines conduct
ærial surveys of a zone
so infinitesimal in scale
that it exists as a texture
without surface, a ripple
without water, the photo
showing us the stillness
of wind trapped within
the silkiness of its space.

FIGURE 2.6: The subatomic topography of glossematics

Spiderwebs are bubbles of soap packed inside a windowpane.

The moiré effect occurs when two lattices with a fine grain
overlap at a slightly skewed angle so that for a few seconds
they produce the illusion of motion amid the fixity of lines.

Sunlight turns a swimming pool into a melting kaleidoscope.

SAPPHIRE

```
                    A
                    L
                    U
                    M
          O         I
        O X Y G E N
          Y         U
        O X Y G E N   M
          E
    A L U M I N U M
```

altazimuth
allure, outshone

oneiric oceanarium

GRAIN BOUNDARIES

```
rim                     rime
          emery
memory              remora
memoir
          moiré
                  mirror
                  mirage
image               regime
          gems
edges               emerge
          energy
elegy               elegant
                    element
letter              stellar
steel
          steam
                    metal
master              sleet
          maelstrom
icestorm            serum
          simulacrum
shimmer             sheer
          meerschaum
echelon             mesh
measure
muse            machinery
```

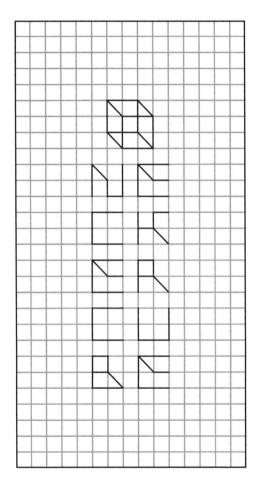

NECKER CUBE

PIEZOELECTRICITY

Crystalline batteries
of electrified quartz
emit ultrasonic songs.

Fireflies materialize
one by one ex nihilo
inside the Leyden jar,
hermetically sealed
in 1754, then thrown
overboard in a storm
by associate members
of the Royal Society.

Flashbulbs and vacuum
tubes – time capsules
of blown glass, minus
content, incandesce
at subaqueous extremes
of compression: soap
bubbles that descend
into will-o'-the-wisps.

Luminosities brighten
as the growing burden
of their depth nears
bathypelagic implosion:
electric eels awaken
the body of a drowned
dolphin to galvanic
life in their embrace.

Watch hearts fibrillate,
their quartz crystals
out of sync with each
second coming (coming)
apart in minute hands,
the stars but asterisks
that ignite when they
reach critical masses.

Television static jolts
clear under the stress
of evening newsflashes:
hyphens, like steel rods
parallel to geomagnetic
fields, turn to magnets
when struck at one end
with a ball-peen hammer.

Sparks, triboluminescent
from prehistoric impacts
of flint, jump-start tools,
like manual typewriters,
into dreams of existence,
each keystroke inducing
an electroshock therapy
in you, unwitting user.

Words are but one-way
mirrors cracked by the
vises of a picture frame.

JADE

```
                        A
                        L
                O       U
                X       M
            O   Y       I
            O X Y G E N
            O   Y   E   U
            O X Y G E N   M
    S   S       E
    I   O X Y G E N
    L   D       E
    S I L I C O N
    C   U
    O   M
    N
```

oriental nachtmusik

opium
ormolu, alalia

octagon

singsong siamang

origami ouijaboard

HOLOSYMMETRY

A euphemism for all
organic unity found
in crystalloidal form.

A synonym for beauty
in a discourse bereft
of æsthetic theories.

A structural tendency
in any form that shifts
to a higher dimension.

A geometric principle
by which nature makes
spherical the cubical.

A figure whose parts
resemble each other
from any perspective.

A portal that opens
like a porthole to link
every part to its whole.

A crystalline spectrum
maps the æsthetic value
of all stylistic paragons
– from isometric order
in classicism to triclinic
disorder in modernism:
the hexakisoctahedron
being most symmetric
of all the crystal habits,
its thirteen rotary axes
& nine reflexive planes,
for its four dozen facets,
rigidest rhyme scheme
– an ideal form driving
insane every scientific
monk who inhabits its
polyhedral cathedrals,
almost every organism
a bilateral construction
divided against itself,
almost every particle
a planet spinning two
times for every sunset.

1

The Catoptriarchs (AD 711–777), a Slavonic sect of Christian gnostics, advocated the Enantiomorphic Heresy, which declared that all earthly existence was but a fleeting reflection in a looking glass unveiled in the gardens of the Heavenly Father. Catoptriarchs expressed their *contemptus mundi* by refusing to gaze upon the world unless it was reflected in a mirror; any disciple of this sect was easily identified by his periscopic obsession with a sheet of silver plating, which he always carried with him in one hand and from which his glance never strayed, even when riding on horseback. Catoptriarchs earned erroneous repute for their narcissism and suffered persecution by the official clergy in Constantinople. Manuscripts written by the Catoptriarchs were almost all destroyed because the Slavonic mirror-writing in these texts was entirely illegible and thus was often mistaken for Satanic speech by monastic archivists, who burnt each book for the blasphemy, not of its theme, but of its style.

René Just-Haüy (1743–1822), a French crystallographer, numbered among the inventory of his scientific library an incunabulum thought to be the Latin transcription of a manuscript originally written by a Catoptriarch. The Latin was enciphered by an anonymous monk, who wrote using an unusual alphabet inspired by the diffraction patterns that sunbeams make when passing through either prisms of rock quartz or layered panes of glass (see FIGURE 2.7). The French Revolution saw the destruction of this book in the fire at Haüy's library, when arsonists stormed the streets and indiscriminately burned any property that might even suggest the lifestyle of an aristocrat.

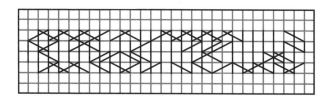

FIGURE 2.7: An alphabet for plotting the transmission
of light rays through a transparent medium

Documentary evidence about the Catoptriarchs survives now only in the fragmentary marginalia scribbled by Haüy in the pages of his private diaries after the fire – diaries in which he not only recounts from memory the above anecdotes, but also reconstructs, as best he can, the prismatic alphabet of his lost text.

2

De Speculum Oraculum (AD 1230), the final volume in a trilogy about medieval glassblowing, now resides deep in the secret repository of forbidden books at the Vatican, since the text allegedly describes heretical techniques for predicting the advent of the Apocalypse. Written on scorched vellum pages, interleaved between polished steel plates, all bound together by solid glass clamps, one at each corner, the text discourses upon the arts of both catoptromancy and crystallomancy – two genres of soothsaying that allow a clairvoyant to foresee the future, to witness the end of the world, by gazing into the hypnotic abysses of either mirrors or crystals.

De Speculum purports to be the vade mecum for a secret guild of German glassblowers supposedly able to manufacture a mirror that can, when smashed, depict a multitude of destinies in its mosaic of fragments, each piece containing a different image, a single scene, from the life of the person last reflected in the glass. The diverse images among the random shards do not appear to have any coherent order so that the clairvoyant must interpret their proper relations within the arrangement. The clairvoyant constructs a narrative from the mosaic, whose images stay visible so long as the pattern of their shattering goes undisturbed, for even a slight movement of the mosaic causes them to disappear, never to return.

De Speculum concludes with a natural history of crystals, complete with diagrams. The book alludes to a theory of optics, in which the pathways of light through a jewel embody the pathways of thought through the mind so that optical reflection provides an allegory for cerebral reflection. The book goes on to warn that gazing into a perfect crystal for too long can cause the soul of the clairvoyant to become trapped irrevocably within the faceted depths of the gem. The imprisonment of the soul in this way causes the clairvoyant to go insane, and destruction of the gem results in the immediate death of the imprisoned victim. The text predicts that the world ends when men lose their minds by emptying their memories into mirrors in the same way that scribes write messages upon a page.

3

Christian Weiss (1780–1856), a German crystallographer, recounts in a love letter to his mistress the following curious anecdote about a discovery that he made during his research on crystalline symmetry at the Berlin Academy.

Weiss reports purchasing a medieval treatise on the use of mirrors in the game of chess – a treatise that he found at an antiquarian bookstall on the verge of the ghetto. Weiss writes that the prolegomenon of the book chronicles the apocryphal experiments of a Saracen alchemist reputed to have made items vanish by placing them between a tall pair of looking glasses erected in the court of his patron, the Caliph.

Double mirrors facing each other can, according to this book, trap the spirits of the dead who pass between them; moreover, any living person who has no soul can step into either one of the mirrors as if it were an open door and thus walk down the illusory corridor that appears to recede forever into the depths of the glass by virtue of one mirror reflecting itself in the other. The walls of such a corridor are said to be made from invulnerable panes of crystal, beyond which lies a nullified dimension of such complexity that to view it is surely to go insane. The book also explains at length that, after an eternity of walking down such a corridor, a person eventually exits from the looking glass opposite to the one first entered.

Weiss speculates that a soulless man might carry another pair of mirrors into such a corridor, thereby producing a hallway at right angles to the first one. Such a man might, of course, perform this procedure again and again in any of the corridors until he has erected an endless labyrinth of glass inside the first pair of mirrors, each mirror opening onto an extensive grid of crisscrossing hallways, some of which never intersect, despite their lengths being both infinite and perpendicular. Weiss expresses his own misgivings about becoming hopelessly lost while exploring such a maze, and he wonders what happens to the prisoner if the initial pair of mirrors are disturbed so that they no longer reflect each other, thus suddenly obliterating the fragile foundation upon which the entire maze rests.

Weiss never divulges the title of this bizarre treatise, and since no one has ever corroborated the existence of such a book, literary scholars have simply dismissed this anecdote as an elaborate falsehood, designed to entertain his mistress, a countess rumoured to have grown easily bored with any lover unable to appease her intellectual appetite for enigmas, puzzles and rebuses.

4

Rev Charles Lutwidge Dodgson (1832–1898), a British mathematician, wrote about his experiments with hallucinogenic drugs, recording his experiences on some pages tipped into a single copy of the first edition of his treatise on geometry, *Euclid and His Modern Rivals*, a copy now thought to be in the possession of a private collector in Luxembourg.

Dodgson reported that, while reading the book *Al Aaraaf* during his studies at Christ Church in Oxford, he grew ever more curious about altered states of mental awareness and thus decided to visit a pharmacy where he acquired a dose of crystallized opiates in the hope that he too might experience within the privacy of his own garret the visions of the poetry. Dodgson wrote that, shortly after administering the drug in an infusion of laudanum, he began to feel an ominous anxiety while contemplating the halo of light rays emanating from a gas lamp in his room, for the rays seemed to grow steadily more distinct, more refined, attenuating themselves into long, slender needles honed to a divine acuity, the lamp transmuting into what he described as 'a silvery thistle of illumination, radiating acicular beams of searing energy that pierced through any object in their path.' Distressed, he stood up suddenly from his desk and accidentally knocked over a looking glass, only to see it topple in slow motion onto the floor, where the mirror burst into smithereens.

Dodgson claimed that, to his amazement, the glittering fragments of the broken mirror floated up one by one into the air, each a spinning prism that began to orbit elliptically around his head and body at an accelerated rate until all the shards formed a kind of kaleidoscopic shield that deflected the sharpened beams of gaslight. Dodgson, euphoric, described himself later as 'a tree surrounded by its nimbus of silver leaves when the wind shivers them to life.' Mesmerized, he attempted to step out through this cyclonic barrier of flying shrapnel, only to faint when the light rays pierced him at every point and the bladed shards of glass sliced him to shreds. Dodgson awoke, uninjured, hours later beside his broken mirror and promptly recorded the hallucination in his journal, but then decided to keep his experience secret for fear of being diagnosed as deranged by his academic colleagues, who thought him a bit queer for befriending pubescent girls by composing for them nonsensical verse.

5

Jacques Lacan (1901–1981), a French psychoanalyst, first delivered his seminal essay 'The Mirror Stage as Formative of the Function of the I' on July 17, 1946, while attending the Sixteenth International Congress of Psychoanalysis in Zürich. Lacan upheld the idea that an infant in the first months of its life could only apprehend the experience of both self and other via *méconnaissance*, the child misconstruing itself as other when seeing its own reflection in a mirror for the first time. Lacan argued that this developmental stage induced a crisis of alienation, since the subject defined itself through an external image, whose ideality could never coincide exactly with the identity of the child. Because of this irreconcilable distance between the subject and its reflection, the child not only admired its own image for providing a coherent representation of the self, but also despised its own image for withholding a representation congruent with the self. Lacan concluded that this psychodrama marked the transition of a subject from a state of lack to a state of desire.

Le Monde reported in its morning edition on the same day as this academic symposium that Dr Jules Verrier, a clinical psychiatrist, had gone insane while trying to escape from an elevator that had trapped him alone overnight between the floors of his office building. Verrier had apparently screamed for almost seven hours straight, all the while clawing away at the mirrored interior of his compartment, before firemen finally rescued him and escorted him away under restraint. Sources close to the scene testified later that the psychiatrist had behaved quite hysterically, insisting to authorities that he had become involved in a case of mistaken identity, that he was the wrong person taken into custody, since his reflection in the mirrored wall of the elevator had somehow traded places with him. His reflection had suddenly refused to imitate him and had stepped out of its frame so as to force him to occupy the space vacated in the glass.

Verrier was committed a day later to L'Hôpital Général in Paris, where doctors tried to console him by telling him that obviously he was not imprisoned in a mirror, but he responded to treatment by yelling in frustration that nobody understood him, for he insisted that this world was itself the very world beyond the mirror, a world from which his reflection had escaped, tearing itself free so as to wreak havoc upon the true reality. Medical authorities at the asylum diagnosed the patient as a paranoid catoptrophobiac, but confessed ironically that they now preferred to exit buildings via the stairs.

NOTES

Crystalline forms that mirror each other through an axis of symmetry are called *enantiomers;* for example, a vertical axis makes enantiomers not only of *b* and *d,* but also of *p* and *q,* just as a horizontal axis makes enantiomers not only of *b* and *p,* but also of *d* and *q.* Words form enantiomers of each other only when one translates into the other through reflection.

Enantiomers can also occur when two crystals undergo the process of interpenetrant twinning; for example, *w* takes shape at the moment when *v* twins with its enantiomer through a vertical axis, just as *X* takes shape at the moment when *v* twins with its enantiomer through a horizontal axis. Such symmetries underlie the order of all crystalline forms.

Mirrors have historically provided a mathematical means for identifying a crystalline structure on the basis of its internal symmetries. A scientist determines the class of symmetry to which a crystal belongs by slicing the crystal along diverse axes with a mirrored blade. The reflections in the blade define the degree to which the crystal is symmetrical with itself.

Even a palindrome is a kind of enantiomer; for example, the phrase *mirror rim* reveals a sequential symmetry, in which the order of letters in one direction repeats itself when reversed. Each letter is also catoptric in its own structure: the doubled *r,* doubled, the letters *m, i* and *o,* each symmetrical through a vertical axis, the gap between the two words a flaw in the gem.

MIRRORS INDUCE DYSLEXIA

CRYSTAL SYSTEM	SYMMETRY AXIS				CRYSTAL STRUCTURE
	DIA	TRI	TET	HEX	
1. TRICLINIC	–	–	–	–	F G J L P Q R
2. MONOCLINIC	1	–	–	–	A M T U V W, B C D E K, N S Z
3. ORTHORHOMBIC	3	–	–	–	H I
4. ISOMETRIC	(6)	4	(3)	–	–
5. TRIGONAL	(3)	1	–	–	Y
6. TETRAGONAL	(4)	–	1	–	O X
7. HEXAGONAL	(6)	–	–	1	–

Unbracketed numerals indicate the mandatory number of axes required for a crystal to occupy a given system. Bracketed numerals indicate the maximum number of optional axes within such a system.

FIGURE 2.8: A table of crystal systems for classifying letters of the alphabet on the basis of axial symmetry

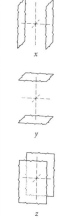

The axis of symmetry describes a mathematical line that passes through the centre of any crystal such that rotation about this line through an arc of $360°/n$ (where $n \in I$) causes the crystal to assume a final position congruent with its initial position. For $n = 1$, the crystal can achieve self-congruence by rotating 360° around an *identity* axis; for $n = 2$, the crystal can achieve self-congruence by rotating 180° around a *diad* axis; for $n = 3$, the crystal can achieve self-congruence by rotating 120° around a *triad* axis; for $n = 4$, the crystal can achieve self-congruence by rotating 90° around a *tetrad* axis; and for $n = 6$, the crystal can achieve self-congruence by rotating 60° around a *hexad* axis. No crystal exists with axes of symmetry for $n = 5$ or for $n > 6$.

The number of such axes of symmetry in a given letter determines the crystal system to which the letter belongs: the crystal H, for example, coincides with itself when rotated 180° through any one of three different orientations, and thus the letter belongs to the orthorhombic system, whose members typically have three such diad axes. The alphabet consists predominantly of monoclinic crystals, three types, all having a single diad axis of symmetry: a) three letters symmetrical only through the x-axis; b) five letters symmetrical only through the y-axis; and c) six letters symmetrical only through the z-axis. The triclinic system, the next most common system in the alphabet, contains letters with no axis of symmetry other than their infinite number of identity axes.

The science of crystallography suggests that both the isometric system and the hexagonal system do occur in nature; however, no poet searching throughout the world of language has yet discovered a letter that fits into either system – a mystery that has led some crystallographers to speculate that crystals expressing such a rare degree of symmetry can only exist under the most extreme poetic conditions: perhaps the low temperatures found only in the voids of outer space or the high pressures found only in the cores of neutron stars – conditions difficult for writers to reproduce in the laboratory.

TOPAZ

```
             F
   A         L
 A L U M I N U M
   U         O
   M         R
   I       S I L I C O N
   N         N       X
 F L U O R I N E   O X Y G E N
   M               X   G
                 O X Y G E N
                   G   N
                   E
                   N
```

alexandrine ortolan

orangutan

sinhalese fantasia

onomastic
otacoustic

almandine, farewell

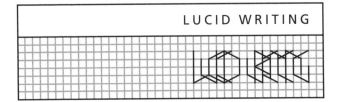

LUCID WRITING

Crystallography is a pataphysical encyclopædia that misreads the language of poetics through the conceits of geology. While the word 'crystallography' quite literally means 'lucid writing,' this book does not concern itself with the transparent transmission of a message (so that, ironically, much of the poetry may seem 'opaque'); instead, the book concerns itself with the reflexive operation of its own process (in a manner that might call to mind the surreal poetics of lucid dreaming).

The first edition of this book was published by the old Coach House Press in 1994. When Margaret McClintock, the editor, accepted the book for publication, she admitted that no one in her office had the skill to typeset such an unorthodox manuscript. Surprised that a press renowned for the quality of its design could no longer call upon the talents of its traditional typesetters, I brazenly declared that, if necessary, I would teach myself the software and set the book myself.

Crystallography appeared in print only because my friend Katy Chan, a designer, donated weeks of her own expertise to this meticulous enterprise, letting me supervise while she did the layout on my behalf. We dragooned friends into trimming by hand more than one thousand acetate tip-ins, the cost of which I absorbed because the publisher could not afford it. We also faced many frustrating limitations in the software used, and often we had to resort to makeshift solutions.

The second edition of this book attempts to redress some of these intractable typographic problems that went unresolved in the original printing. Since the work predicates itself upon an æsthetics of structural perfection, these deficiencies, although minor, have often caused me private concern. Most improvements incorporate changes proposed in 1994 by Katy Chan, but never executed by her because of economic decisions and logistic deadlines imposed by the publisher.

Wherever possible, I have streamlined the design for the sake of a much cleaner, much tighter look. Typos have been corrected. Poems once crowded onto a single page in order to limit the length of the work have expanded to fill more space. I have altered the layout of some pieces in order to accomodate the parameters of the new font, and a few weaker poems have undergone either excision (if their presence seems extraneous) or revision (if their presence seems obligatory).

Support for this book has been provided over the years by many friends: Charles Bernstein, Stan Bevington, Katy Chan, jwcurry, Christopher Dewdney, Kenneth Goldsmith, Michael Holmes, Carl Johnston, Bill Kennedy, Karen Mac Cormack, Steve McCaffery, Ming-Qian Ma, Marjorie Perloff, Matthew Remski, Rick/Simon, Natasha Stewart and Alana Wilcox. Many thanks to Darren Wershler-Henry (for his dilithium crystals) and to Natalee Caple (for her nighttime emeralds).

Excerpts from this book have appeared in the following publications: *Acta Victoriana, The Capilano Review, Descant, The Globe and Mail, Industrial Sabotage, The Instant Anthology, One Cent, Oversion, PUSHYbroadsides, Rampike, Sin Over Tan, Torque, U. C. Review, Virus 23, The Last Word* (Insomniac Press, 1995), *Blues and True Concussions* (House of Anansi Press, 1996), *Imagining Language* (MIT Press, 1998) and *Imaginary Numbers* (John Wiley & Sons, 1999).

Some poems have been written with friends in mind: 'Diamonds' is dedicated to Carl Johnston; '[Triptych]' is dedicated to Natasha Stewart; 'Midwinter Glaciaria' is dedicated to Christopher Dewdney; and the revised version of 'Geodes' is dedicated to Natalee Caple. The frontispiece, entitled 'The Glass Harmonica,' is a collage superimposed upon the score for 'Adagio and Rondo in C Minor, K. 617' by Mozart, one of the few concertos written for crystal goblets filled with water.

Christian Bök is the author of *Eunoia* (Coach House Books, 2001), a bestselling work of experimental literature, which has won the Griffin Prize for Poetic Excellence (2002). *Crystallography* (Coach House Press, 1994), his first book of poetry, earned a nomination for the Gerald Lampert Memorial Award (1995). Bök has created artificial languages for two television shows: Gene Roddenberry's *Earth: Final Conflict* and Peter Benchley's *Amazon*. Bök has earned many accolades for his virtuoso performances of sound poetry (particularly the *Ursonate* by Kurt Schwitters). His conceptual artworks (which include books built out of Rubik's Cubes and Lego) have appeared at the Marianne Boesky Gallery in New York as part of the exhibit *Poetry Plastique*. He teaches creative writing at the University of Calgary.

Typeset in Minion and Frutiger. Printed and bound
at Coach House Printing on bpNichol Lane, 2003

EDITOR
Alana Wilcox

DESIGNER
Christian Bök

COPYEDITOR
Alana Wilcox

Read the online version of this text at our website: www.chbooks.com

Send us a request to be added to our mailing list:
mail@chbooks.com

Call us toll-free:
1 800 367 6360

Coach House Books
401 Huron Street (rear) on bpNichol Lane
Toronto, Ontario
M5S 2G5